....'s

Long Life

RP Studio™
Hachette Book Group
1290 Avenue of the Americas, New York, NY 10104
www.runningpress.com
@Running_Press

Printed in China

First Edition: December 2022

Perseus Books, LLC, a subsidiary of Hachette Book Group, Inc. The RP Studio name and logo is a trademark of the Hachette Book Group.

The publisher is not responsible for websites (or their content) that are not owned by the publisher.

Design by Jenna McBride

ISBN: 978-0-7624-8117-0

APS

10 9 8 7 6 5 4 3 2 1

MY LONG LIFE

A GUIDED JOURNAL FOR DESIGNING A LIFE OF LOVE, PURPOSE, WELL-BEING, AND FRIENDSHIP AT ANY AGE

WRITTEN AND ILLUSTRATED BY AYSE BIRSEL

RP STUDIO

PHILADELPHIA

INTRODUCTION

The other night, my teenage daughter said to me, "You have another forty to fifty years to live, Mom—as much as you've already lived. This is very exciting!"

Thinking about a long life is very exciting indeed. It's also a new phenomenon. Fifty years ago, people rarely lived past their sixties. Living into one's seventies was considered the mark of a long life. Today, seventy feels young, eighty feels normal, and ninety is within reach.

This changes everything for all of us. Gen Xers, millennials, postmillennials, boomers.

If we are the first people to have a lot more time on this planet, how do we want to live those extra years? Who do we want to be now? What do we want going forward? What brings us joy? What is the purpose of our lives?

This new horizon of life is as important and exciting as the invention of moving pictures. Or that of automobiles, or even space travel. My point is, when a change this big happens, innovation follows.

When it comes to our lives, we are our own innovators—so let's begin to learn how to do just that. *Prepare to design your long life!*

DESIGNING
YOUR
LONG LIFE

It all began with a simple idea. I believe life itself is our biggest project. And as a designer, I decided to test this idea by applying my design thinking process, Deconstruction:Reconstruction, to life. From this idea, I began Design the Life You Love as an experiment in 2010.

I was my first test subject. I created exercises and tried them out. Then I tried them on my friends. My friends told their friends, and the whole thing grew by word of mouth—suddenly, lots of people were designing the lives they loved. Linda Tischler, then the senior design editor of *Fast Company*, wrote about my method in *Huffington Post*. She called the piece "Forget New Year's Resolutions.

This Year, Use Design Tools to Redesign Your Life," and that put the idea on the map.

As a designer, I've created many things in my life. No one has ever written to me to say, "I love your potato-peeler for Target," or "I love your office system for Herman Miller." But they do tell me that designing their life in this way has been transformative. That feedback is why I love teaching people how to design their lives.

It's especially helpful to think about what goes into creating a meaningful long life—after all, living for a long time is such a fresh concept!

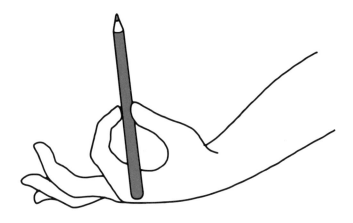

Through my work codesigning with older adults, I've found that a fulfilling long life is based on the four pillars of Love, Purpose, Well-Being, and Friendship. With the help of this journal, those guiding principles, and the tools of design, you can create your own long, meaningful, and original life, no matter your age.

One of the reasons why designing your life is so transformational is simple. It has something to do with the tools of design: pen and paper. When you draw, sketch, write, or take notes, you connect your internal thoughts to the outside world. You can focus, ponder, sleep on, come back to, move forward, and improve on an idea that is visible.

Cognitive science tells us there is a direct correlation between the brain and the hand. Throughout this journal, I will ask you to draw as well as write about your ideas, insights, and feelings. Writing and drawing will allow you to think about the same things differently. It will make 1+1=3.

Often, people worry about their drawing skills. Let me put that to rest. Did you draw when you were a kid? You probably learned how to use a pen before you could use a fork. Then rest assured: that is the level of drawing you can use for design. Channel your inner child. Stick figures, emojis, and maps are more than sufficient in the following pages.

To imagine, use your pen. Let's get started!

1.

DRAWING A PERSON CONNECTS YOUR IDEA
TO PEOPLE, TO LIFE, TO HUMANITY.

2.

SIMPLE SHAPES DEPICT AN IDEA,
A SPACE, OR A CATEGORY.

3.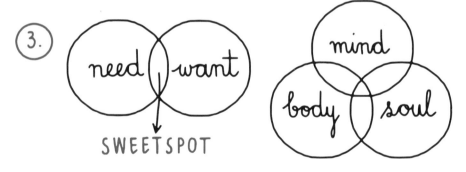

TWO OVERLAPPING CIRCLES DEPICT
INTERSECTING IDEAS OR A DICHOTOMY
RESOLUTION. THREE — MULTIPLE
IDEAS, CRITERIA, OR CHOICES.

4.

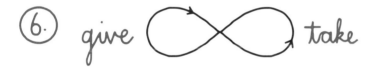

DRAWING A GRAPH REPRESENTS THE
RELATIONSHIP OF ONE THING TO ANOTHER.

5. $+ \; - \; \times \; / \; = \; \neq \; < \; > \; \% \; |+| = 3$

MATH SYMBOLS ALSO REPRESENT
RELATIONSHIP OF ONE THING TO ANOTHER.

6. give ∞ take

INFINITY SIGN OR LOOPS DEPICT
RECIPROCITY OR INTERDEPENDANCE.

7.

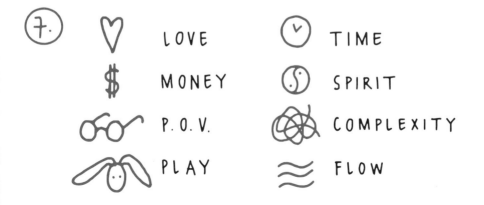

♡ LOVE

$ MONEY

👓 P.O.V.

PLAY

TIME

SPIRIT

COMPLEXITY

FLOW

Let's start our design with thinking creatively about Love. The people and things we love give us joy. Here are things that give me joy—a parade of clouds on a blue sky, a cup of hot Earl Grey tea, great art, a good book, and you, dear reader, who are holding this journal in your hand.

What brings me joy?

a parade of clouds

a cup of hot tea

Olafur Eliasson's art

a good book

and, you!

draw

write

now, your turn!

Now you try. Draw some things that bring you joy.

What brings me joy

_____   _____

_____   _____

_____   _____

To warm up your creative brain, draw something—fruit, your coffee cup, dog, cat, children—for five to ten minutes. Just draw. Don't judge and don't erase.

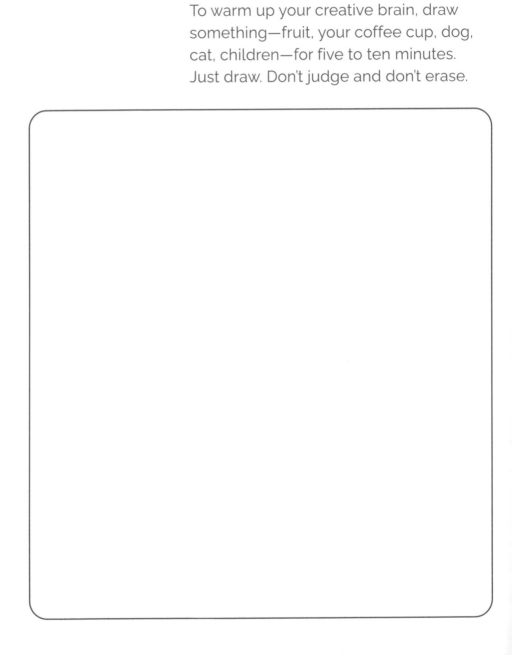

Draw something on your desk (e.g., your stapler) in five minutes, without looking at your hand. Cover your hand with a paper towel to help you not cheat. When done, take away the towel. Ta-da! You'll be amazed.

Now that you're comfortable drawing, let's start the journey of designing your long life by thinking about design itself.

Are you optimistic? Do you have empathy for other people? Do you like having a bird's-eye view of things? Do you overuse the words *what if*? Do you enjoy collaborating with others? If so, you're already thinking like a designer.

Optimism—the belief that we will find a better solution no matter how hard the problem—fuels our energy, calms our fears, and propels us forward. Write about a time when you were optimistic. Draw how it made you feel (emojis welcome).

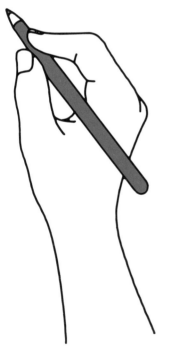

A designer's empathy is human-centered.
We put ourselves in other people's shoes
to understand what they need and want.
Draw yourself and a person you are feel-
ing empathy for (stick-figures are okay!).
Write what they are feeling.

We think holistically to see the big picture, read the patterns, and connect the dots in new and different ways. How about you? Write or draw a bird's-eye view of something that is at the top of your mind. What is a pattern that is emerging?

We ask *what-if* questions, knowing our answers often come from unexpected, counterintuitive places. What are some *what-if* questions that are on your mind right now?

_____

_____

_____

_____

_____

_____

_____

_____

_____

_____

_____

_____

_____

_____

_____

_____

_____

_____

We (designers and everyone) love to collaborate so that we can learn from each other, to inspire and build on each other's ideas. Write about the last time you collaborated with others. You can also draw them and map out the give and take that exists between you (arrows and idea bubbles are fun here).

_____

_____

_____

_____

_____

_____

_____

_____

_____

_____

_____

_____

_____

_____

_____

_____

_____

_____

Being playful is the mood of design. When we're playing, we're like kids—unafraid to make mistakes. Write about or draw the last time you let yourself truly play.

This rabbit is your reminder to be playful when you design.

_____

_____

_____

_____

_____

_____

_____

_____

_____

_____

_____

Now that you're thinking like a designer and have thought about Love, let's think about what gives our lives shape and structure. Let's deep dive into exploring our sense of Purpose.

When we're younger, we derive our sense of purpose from well-defined organizations, like school, office, home, or places of worship. I call these *ready-made purpose*. These structures lose their importance, recede, or disappear in later life as we retire or have second careers, become empty-nesters, or downsize. Our sense of purpose starts to come from within, which I call *self-made purpose*. Self-made purpose includes things like volunteering, fighting for a cause you believe in, and honing your creativity.

Ready- or self-made, our purpose is a continuum. Deriving meaning from what we do has no age. What are examples of ready-made purpose in your life? What about examples of self-made purpose?

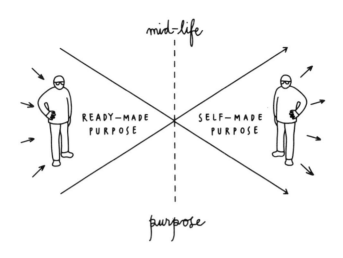

mid-life

READY—MADE
PURPOSE

SELF—MADE
PURPOSE

purpose

_____
_____
_____
_____
_____
_____
_____
_____
_____
_____
_____
_____
_____
_____
_____
_____
_____

When we're students and our life is mostly about going to school . . . *we work to learn*. When we leave school, look for a job, and start working . . . *we learn to work*. As we take on new responsibilities, like having a family or taking care of our elders, our work and life become one . . . *we live to work*. As we grow older and become wiser, doing what we love, helping others, and being kind to ourselves, purpose becomes more important and . . . *we work to live our best lives*.

Part of the wisdom that comes from experience is realizing you don't have to wait to be older to do what you love. You can be intentional about being the master of your time. You can lean into your expertise. You can help others— helping others helps us. You can practice reciprocity—teach and learn, help and be helped, give and take.

These are things that come easier to us as we live longer, but why wait until then? Part of designing a life we love is working to live our best lives from early on.

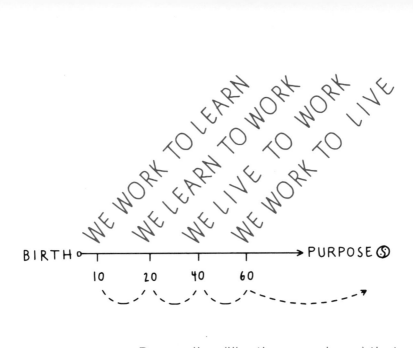

WE WORK TO LEARN
WE LEARN TO WORK
WE LIVE TO WORK
WE WORK TO LIVE

BIRTH o———————→ PURPOSE Ⓢ

10   20   40   60

Draw a line (like the one above) that begins at birth and ends at finding your purpose and map your life of purpose.

Having purpose is about creating meaning. Creating meaning is motivating and energizing. It gets us out of bed every morning. Here are eight ways you can create meaning. Refer to this diagram as you answer the following prompts.

What have you created lately in terms of an art, craft, design, fashion, writing, and/or music? Write or draw about it.

Write about a time when you started something new. Or draw something new that you're thinking about starting.

Write about a time when you fought for what you believed in. What was your rallying cry? Draw a placard!

Write about a time when you taught
someone something.

_____
_____
_____
_____
_____
_____
_____
_____
_____
_____
_____
_____
_____
_____
_____
_____
_____
_____
_____
_____
_____
_____

Write about a time you solved a problem,
or draw a picture of your solution.

Draw yourself as a leader. You can add icons or accessories (road map, treasure box, rocket). Write about what you drew. (Want an extra challenge? Search for the *New York Times* article *Picture a Leader. Is She a Woman?* by Heather Murphy for a terrific read on leadership.)

Write about a time when you served others. You can also draw yourself at the center and add the people you've helped around you.

_____

_____

_____

_____

_____

_____

_____

_____

_____

_____

_____

_____

_____

_____

_____

_____

_____

_____

Write about a time when you learned
something new, or draw a picture of what
you learned about.

"THIS IS YOUR ONE AND PRECIOUS LIFE.

I WANT YOU TO DO SOMETHING WITH IT.

NOT BECAUSE YOU'RE A BAD PERSON IF

YOU DON'T, BUT IF YOU DO, YOU MIGHT

FIND A MORE INTERESTING VERSION

OF YOURSELF, A MORE COMPLETE,

EXPANDED, THRILLING VERSION OF

YOURSELF. AND YOU MIGHT ALSO MAKE

THE WORLD A BIT BETTER FOR YOURSELF,

FOR OTHERS, AND FOR ME. IF I'VE GOT A

LOT OF PEOPLE DOING WORTHY GOALS,

THE WORLD'S GOING TO BE

A BIT BETTER AS A RESULT OF THAT."

—MICHAEL BUNGAY STANIER, AUTHOR OF *HOW TO BEGIN*

The work that brings us joy sits between creating more time to do what we love and having less time to waste; having more experience, expertise, and wisdom while caring less about what others think.

_____

_____

_____

_____

_____

_____

_____

_____

_____

_____

_____

_____

_____

_____

_____

_____

_____

_____

In what ways do you care what others think? Can you let some of those cares go? How will that free up your time?

What other ways do you make meaning
out of your life?

_____

_____

_____

_____

_____

_____

_____

_____

_____

_____

_____

_____

_____

_____

_____

_____

_____

_____

When you ask an active question—"Did I do my best to have clear goals?"—there's no "them." You're not judging anybody else; you're just talking about you. Active questions help us take responsibility for our own lives and sense of meaning, which of course is the foundation of designing an original life.

On the next page, take a look at the Six Daily Questions from Marshall Goldsmith, author of *The Earned Life*. Then, on the pages that follow, keep track of your own progress with each question—give yourself a score of 1/10 on each goal and see how you progress over time!

Did I try my best to ...

- SET CLEAR GOALS
- MAKE PROGRESS TOWARD
    GOAL ACHIEVEMENT
- BE HAPPY
- FIND MEANING
- BUILD POSITIVE RELATIONSHIPS
- BE FULLY ENGAGED

DID I TRY MY BEST TO . . .

Did I try my best to set clear goals?

Did I try my best to make progress toward goal achievement?

Did I try my best to be happy?

Did I try my best to find meaning?

Did I try my best to build positive relationships?

Did I try my best to be fully engaged?

Day 1	Day 2	Day 3	Day 4	Day 5	Day 6	Day 7

Did I try my best to set clear goals?

Did I try my best to make progress toward
goal achievement?

Did I try my best to be happy?

Did I try my best to find meaning?

Did I try my best to build positive relationships?

Did I try my best to be fully engaged?

Day 1	Day 2	Day 3	Day 4	Day 5	Day 6	Day 7

Did I try my best to set clear goals?

Did I try my best to make progress toward
goal achievement?

Did I try my best to be happy?

Did I try my best to find meaning?

Did I try my best to build positive relationships?

Did I try my best to be fully engaged?

Day 1	Day 2	Day 3	Day 4	Day 5	Day 6	Day 7

Did I try my best to set clear goals?

Did I try my best to make progress toward goal achievement?

Did I try my best to be happy?

Did I try my best to find meaning?

Did I try my best to build positive relationships?

Did I try my best to be fully engaged?

Day 1	Day 2	Day 3	Day 4	Day 5	Day 6	Day 7

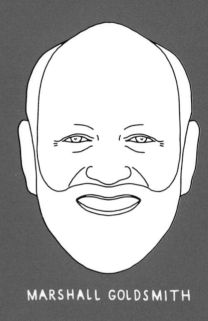

MARSHALL GOLDSMITH

"I'VE LEARNED IT'S NEVER TOO LATE TO REFLECT, BECAUSE AS LONG AS YOU'RE BREATHING YOU HAVE MORE TIME. BUT IT'S NEVER TOO EARLY AS WELL—AND EARLY IS BETTER."

—MARSHALL GOLDSMITH, *THE EARNED LIFE*

Purpose and Well-Being go hand in hand. Well-being is not only external but also internal. It's realizing that helping others is the best way to help yourself. It's exercising a little every day. It's adapting and rolling with the punches and persevering. It's accepting who you are. It's being an optimist and declaring victory over each day.

Let's explore what well-being can look like as you design your long life.

Well-being is both mind and body. How
are you taking care of your mind?

_____

_____

_____

_____

_____

_____

_____

_____

_____

_____

_____

_____

_____

_____

_____

_____

_____

_____

_____

_____

How are you taking care of your body?

_____

_____

_____

_____

_____

_____

_____

_____

_____

_____

_____

_____

_____

_____

_____

_____

_____

_____

_____

_____

_____

_____

_____

What are you grateful for—people and things?

_____

_____

_____

_____

_____

_____

_____

_____

_____

_____

_____

_____

_____

_____

_____

_____

_____

_____

_____

_____

_____

Where's your purpose coming from?

What do you do to be in the present?

_____

_____

_____

_____

_____

_____

_____

_____

_____

_____

_____

_____

_____

_____

_____

_____

_____

_____

_____

_____

_____

_____

Designing your life means creating an authentic life, one in which you can be your true and honest self. This is the essence of well-being, especially as you age. No one understands this better than Ron Carucci, author of *To Be Honest*. Ron explained to me that an important part of living an honest life is reconciling the past with the future. Reconciliation is the ability to face yourself, to acknowledge the places you haven't been honest with or about yourself. And then, choose to be satisfied with who you are, even in the midst of regrets, and live out the future to your fullest, despite whatever is behind you.

This step-by-step process from Ron Carucci, about reconciling your past and future, will help you develop your own sense of well-being:

1. MAKE AN INVENTORY. LIST THE UNRESOLVED PLACES WHERE SOMEONE HURT YOU OR WHERE YOU HURT SOMEONE. THESE MAY BE PLACES IN YOUR LIFE YOU'VE KEPT HIDDEN OR SECRET.

2. CIRCLE THE THREE THAT ARE THE MOST PAINFUL. THESE ARE THE GHOSTS THAT OCCUPY YOUR MIND AND HAUNT YOU THE MOST, ROBBING YOU OF JOY, OR OF FEELING PROUD OR CONFIDENT.

3. PERSONIFY THEM AND WRITE THEM A LETTER. ASK THEM FOR FORGIVENESS OR FORGIVE THEM.

4. LET THEM GO. TELL THESE GHOSTS THEIR SERVICES ARE NO LONGER NEEDED IN YOUR LIFE AND THAT YOU'RE RELEASING THEM.

5. SHARE. READ YOUR LETTERS TO SOMEONE WHO WILL LISTEN WITHOUT OFFERING YOU ADVICE. ALL THEY NEED TO DO IS HOLD THIS SPACE WITH YOU.

6. FEEL FREE. KNOWING YOU'RE NOT THE ONLY PERSON HOLDING THIS PAIN ANYMORE IS POWERFUL. IT'S THE BEGINNING OF THE HEALING PROCESS AND OF YOUR RECONCILIATION.

Follow Ron Carucci's step-by-step process here, to reconcile your past and future.

Now try for yourself. Make an inventory. List the unresolved places where some-one hurt you or where you hurt someone.

Circle the three places that are the most painful. Personify them and write them a letter. Ask them for forgiveness or forgive them. Let them go. Tell these ghosts their services are no longer needed in your life and that you're releasing them.

_____

_____

_____

_____

_____

_____

_____

_____

_____

_____

_____

_____

_____

_____

Fill this space with new people, ideas, and experiences, and resolve not to let the old ghosts come back. Write or draw what you are hoping to fill the space with.

_____
_____
_____
_____
_____
_____
_____
_____
_____
_____
_____
_____
_____
_____
_____
_____
_____
_____
_____
_____
_____
_____

Well-being is also social. To explore it fully, we must explore our Friendships. Different from love, friendships are not found but made.

We all need "fresh" friends in addition to our "old" friends. Social connections are the fabric of a good life.

One of the advantages of a long life is the longevity of our friendships. Social connections are the fabric of a good life and what keeps us tethered to our purpose.

Who are your old friends? Write and draw about them here. What is it about them that makes you want to keep them close?

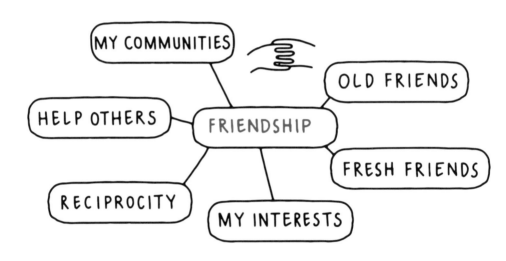

Who are your old friends, and how do you keep them close? Who are your fresh friends, and how do you make them?

_____

_____

_____

_____

_____

_____

_____

_____

_____

_____

_____

_____

_____

_____

_____

_____

_____

_____

_____

Who are your fresh friends? Write and draw here. What was it about them that drew you in?

_____

_____

_____

_____

_____

_____

_____

_____

_____

_____

_____

_____

_____

_____

_____

_____

_____

_____

_____

Lee Kim, who is a design strategist, a mom, and an introvert, has cracked the code on making fresh friends at a time when she too was feeling isolated inside a life that had become too much of a routine. Now, with the process outlined below, she sends out a signal to the world: *Hi! What's your name? You wanna be my friend?*

Here is Lee's step-by-step guide to making fresh friends:

1. PICK YOUR PLAY SPACE. WHEN YOU'RE A KID, THAT SPACE IS THE PLAYGROUND. SAME HERE. FOR LEE, NEW YORK STREETS ARE HER PLAYGROUND.

2. BRING YOUR CONVERSATION STARTER, LIKE YOUR BRIGHT BLUE SAND BUCKET OR FLASHY JUMP ROPE AT THE PLAYGROUND. LEE'S ARE HER DAILY-MADE HATS.

3. GIVE YOURSELF A DURATION. IF YOU'RE LUCKY, YOU GO TO THE PLAYGROUND EVERY DAY, RAIN OR SHINE. LEE GAVE HERSELF 365 DAYS WHEN SHE STARTED HER MISSION TO MAKE NEW FRIENDS.

4. BE PREPARED FOR A CONVERSATION. WHAT IS YOUR "YOU WANNA BE MY FRIEND?" CONVERSATION? LEE TELLS PEOPLE HER HAT STORY AND ASKS THEM WHY THEY THOUGHT IT WAS INTERESTING.

5. KEEP IN TOUCH. IN THE PLAYGROUND, PARENTS EXCHANGE PHONE NUMBERS. LEE ASKS PEOPLE FOR THEIR INSTAGRAM ACCOUNT OR LINKEDIN.

6. GIVE A GIFT. AT THE PLAYGROUND, YOU MIGHT SHARE YOUR CANDY. LEE TAKES OFF HER HAT AND GIFTS IT TO A PERSON EVERY DAY. IT'S THE ULTIMATE INVITATION TO FRIENDSHIP.

Follow Lee Kim's step-by-step process here, for your own version of how you can make fresh friends.

1. PICK A SPACE

2. HAVE A CONVERSATION STARTER

3. GO RAIN OR SHINE

4. BE READY FOR A CONVERSATION

5. KEEP IN TOUCH

6. GIVE A GIFT

What are your play spaces for making fresh friends? What are your conversation starters? And what is something you want to gift to strangers? Something that comes from your heart—a poem, a photo, a hat, a flower, a lesson?

_____

_____

_____

_____

_____

_____

_____

_____

_____

_____

_____

_____

_____

_____

_____

_____

_____

_____

Friends can teach us so much about life—and what we want from our own long lives. This is especially true of friends who aren't just like you. One way to expand your perspective is to seek out friends who are older and younger than you are—nine years in either direction if you can! Are your friends multigenerational—that is to say, are some years younger and some years older than you?

_____

_____

_____

_____

_____

_____

_____

_____

_____

_____

_____

_____

_____

−9   YOUR AGE   +9

friendship formula

What are your shared interests with your friends?

What's the reciprocity principle in your friendship?

_____

_____

_____

_____

_____

_____

_____

_____

_____

_____

_____

_____

_____

_____

_____

_____

_____

_____

_____

_____

_____

_____

What are your communities —family, friends, classmates, work, religion, shared interests, and others?? Write or draw about them here.

_____

_____

_____

_____

_____

_____

_____

_____

_____

_____

_____

_____

_____

_____

_____

_____

_____

_____

_____

What do you do to help others?

"WHETHER YOU'RE AN INTROVERT OR EXTROVERT, THERE HAS TO BE A THRESHOLD THAT YOU HAVE TO CROSS BY CREATING SOMETHING TO SHARE, WHETHER IT'S A SENTENCE, A HAT, OR JUST ARRANGING SOMETHING AND TAKING A PICTURE, TO CONNECT WITH SOMEONE."

—LEE KIM

After trying Lee's step-by-step guide to making fresh friends, write about the experience. Is there anything you would do differently next time?

_____

_____

_____

_____

_____

_____

_____

_____

_____

_____

_____

_____

_____

_____

_____

_____

_____

_____

When we respect each other, including our differences, we are at our most human and can get the most out of our long lives. Equal, equitable, empathic. In what ways are you and your friends different from each other? Apply this question to multiple friendships.

LOVE

 PURPOSE

 WELL-BEING

 FRIENDSHIP

Now that you've learned to think like a designer and have explored Love, Purpose, Well-Being, and Frienship, let's apply what you've learned to the process of designing your long life. To begin, have you had any "a-ha's" or insights?

_____

_____

_____

_____

_____

_____

_____

_____

_____

_____

_____

_____

_____

_____

_____

_____

We are the superheroes of our long lives, with our superpower and kryptonite. Our superpowers are things that come easily to us. Our kryptonite is things that slow us down or deplete our superpowers.

Your superpowers may be curiosity, dealing with chaos, patience, or kindness. Your kryptonite may be a lack of focus, impatience, self-doubt, or procrastination. Sometimes they're the same thing—empathy is a great trait, but if we become consumed by someone else's problems, it is exhausting.

Be intentional about using your superpowers, and don't beat yourself up for having kryptonite. They are both part of who we are. The longer we live, the better we get at accepting our humanness.

Draw yourself as the superhero of your long life.

List your superpowers. These are things that come easily to you.

_____

_____

_____

_____

_____

_____

_____

_____

_____

_____

_____

_____

_____

_____

_____

_____

_____

_____

_____

_____

_____

List your kryptonite. These are things that slow you down.

_____

_____

_____

_____

_____

_____

_____

_____

_____

_____

_____

_____

_____

_____

_____

_____

_____

_____

_____

_____

_____

_____

_____

In life, our design inspiration is other people. These are people we know or we know of. I call them our heroes. Our heroes tell us something about our values, beliefs, and the kind of life we aspire to live.

Who are your older heroes who inspire you? Draw them or write about them.

_____
_____
_____
_____
_____
_____
_____
_____
_____
_____
_____
_____
_____
_____
_____
_____

The qualities we see in our heroes are our own values. That's why we notice them. They can be things like constant evolution, perseverance, having your own voice, longevity, being the best at what you love, and laughing in the face of challenges.

Values are the foundations of our ideas, whether we're designing a chair or our lives. They help us make choices and create something that matters to us. Asking you to gather inspiration from your older heroes was my way of asking you, "What are your values around long life?" Now that you know, you can start practicing them today.

What are the qualities and characteristics that inspire you about your heroes from the previous page? List these with as much detail as possible.

_____

_____

_____

_____

_____

_____

_____

_____

_____

_____

_____

_____

_____

_____

_____

_____

_____

_____

What would you like to do to be
more like your heroes, both now and
in the future?

_____

_____

_____

_____

_____

_____

_____

_____

_____

_____

_____

_____

_____

_____

_____

_____

_____

_____

_____

_____

Constraints are opportunities. That small apartment you've been complaining about is easy to clean. Your long commute is precious alone time. Asking for help is an opportunity for making friends. How can you think of the constraints in your life as opportunities?

_____

_____

_____

_____

_____

_____

_____

_____

_____

_____

_____

_____

_____

_____

_____

_____

_____

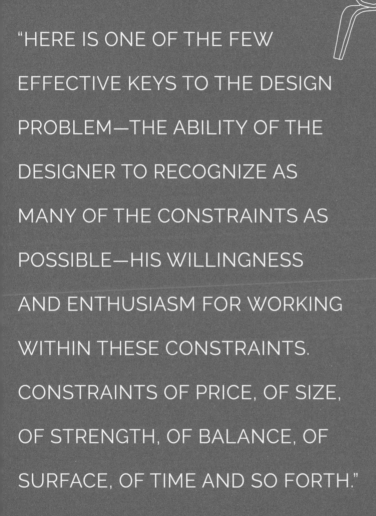

"HERE IS ONE OF THE FEW EFFECTIVE KEYS TO THE DESIGN PROBLEM—THE ABILITY OF THE DESIGNER TO RECOGNIZE AS MANY OF THE CONSTRAINTS AS POSSIBLE—HIS WILLINGNESS AND ENTHUSIASM FOR WORKING WITHIN THESE CONSTRAINTS. CONSTRAINTS OF PRICE, OF SIZE, OF STRENGTH, OF BALANCE, OF SURFACE, OF TIME AND SO FORTH."

—CHARLES EAMES, ICONIC AMERICAN DESIGNER

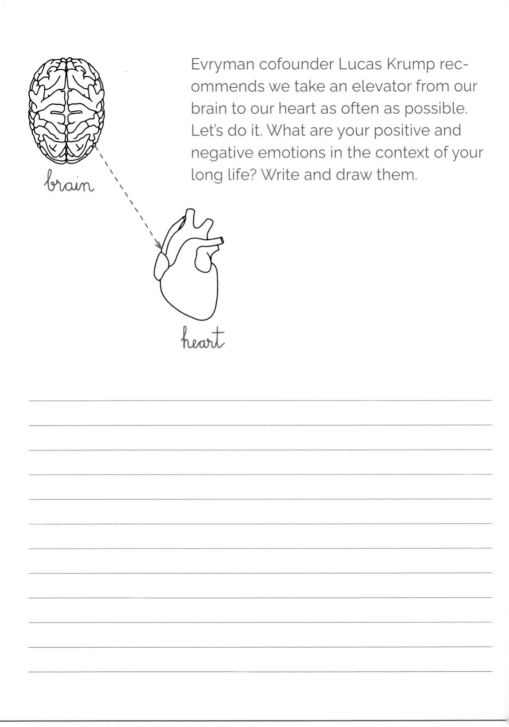

brain

Evryman cofounder Lucas Krump rec-
ommends we take an elevator from our
brain to our heart as often as possible.
Let's do it. What are your positive and
negative emotions in the context of your
long life? Write and draw them.

heart

As you design your long life, I am sure you've come across things you wish weren't there.

We all have them—vices, conflicts, fears. What do you want to avoid in the context of your long life?

_____

_____

_____

_____

_____

_____

_____

_____

_____

_____

_____

_____

_____

_____

_____

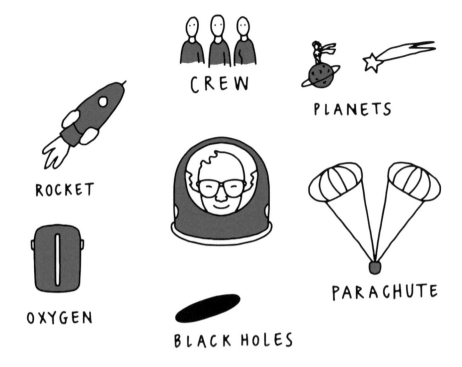

ROCKET

CREW

PLANETS

OXYGEN

PARACHUTE

BLACK HOLES

A good metaphor can help break our old preconceptions and help us see things from a new and different angle. I like to think of those living a long life as astronauts—because they're charting new territory. To explore this idea of being an astronaut of life, going where no one has gone before, think of space travel, real (SpaceX) or fictional (*Star Trek*, *Star Wars*).

How do you prepare for this journey?

What are your superpowers that will help you be a great astronaut of long life?

_____

_____

_____

_____

_____

_____

_____

_____

_____

_____

_____

_____

_____

_____

_____

_____

_____

_____

_____

_____

_____

_____

Draw your rocket. Where do you draw your energy from?

Draw your space suit. What is your suit made of? What protects you and helps you adapt to different environments? What is your oxygen tank, your life source?

Who is your flight crew on this space travel? What are their roles and how do you complement each other?

_____

_____

_____

_____

_____

_____

_____

_____

_____

_____

_____

_____

_____

_____

_____

_____

_____

_____

_____

_____

Draw yourself as the astronaut of your long life. Write down the things that the metaphor conjures up in your imagination.

You can play with this metaphor and add new, fun hooks to expand on your idea. Hooks like discovering new planets, managing limited resources, defending against hostile attacks, and time travel.

Living is also being in a constant state of transition. Metamorphosis is how a caterpillar (past) builds a chrysalis or cocoon (present) to become a butterfly (future). What is your metamorphosis? What are things you want to keep from before (caterpillar stage)? What are things you want to change and/or get rid of (chrysalis stage)? What are your wings to help you take off (butterfly stage)?

_____

_____

_____

_____

_____

_____

_____

_____

_____

_____

_____

_____

_____

caterpillar   chrysalis   butterfly

METAMORPHOSIS

Bill Carrier is a top executive leadership coach. He taught me this powerful self-compassion exercise that reprograms your brain to love yourself. At the end of each day, tell yourself, "I love you." Do this for a minimum of twenty-one days, until it becomes a habit.

Bill says it takes twenty-one days for the brain to reprogram itself—if you skip one day, you need to restart. His suggestion is to combine it with another existing habit, like brushing your teeth, which will help you remember it.

loving yourself

How to teach your brain to love yourself:

STAND IN FRONT OF THE MIRROR RIGHT BEFORE YOU GO
TO BED.

LOOK YOURSELF IN THE EYE AND SAY, "I LOVE YOU."

LIST ALL THE LITTLE AND BIG THINGS YOU'VE
ACCOMPLISHED TODAY.

SAY, "GOOD JOB!"

SAY, "I LOVE YOU, [INSERT YOUR NAME HERE]."

REPEAT FOR A MINIMUM OF TWENTY-ONE DAYS, THE
AMOUNT OF TIME IT SHOULD TAKE FOR THIS TO BECOME
A HABIT.

After telling yourself "I love you" for twenty-one days, write about the experience. How did you feel before? How do you feel now?

_____

_____

_____

_____

_____

_____

_____

_____

_____

_____

_____

_____

_____

_____

_____

_____

_____

_____

_____

At the end of the twenty-one days, write about how your sense of self has changed.

_____

_____

_____

_____

_____

_____

_____

_____

_____

_____

_____

_____

_____

_____

_____

_____

_____

_____

_____

_____

_____

Now let's put the parts of our long life back together, knowing we cannot have everything.

To reconstruct, you need to pick your essentials, the essence of what you love, and leave out the things that are not necessary or are to be avoided. What have you learned is essential for you? What should you avoid? Leaf through your journal for quick reminders.

_____

_____

_____

_____

_____

_____

_____

_____

_____

_____

_____

_____

_____

_____

must have

_____

_____

_____

must avoid

_____

_____
_____
_____
_____
_____
_____
_____
_____
_____
_____
_____
_____
_____

Most of us grew up with a road map our parents gave us—study hard, go to college, find work, work hard, get married, have children, retire. I am oversimplifying, but you get the idea.

Today, this road map doesn't really exist, especially not for long life, since these years didn't really exist before.

Not having a road map is an incredible challenge, but you now know that challenges are our opportunities. The opportunity is to imagine our original road maps. Ones that truly reflect who we are and what we want and need.

Let's imagine our road maps—with bridges and roads, idea factories and collaboration cafés, dragons to slay, and guardian angels to guide us.

Here are icons and labels to help you get started:

- BRIDGES AND ROADS THAT CONNECT THINGS
- IDEA FACTORIES, CARAVANS OF CURIOSITY, COLLABORATION CAFÉS WHERE THINGS GET MADE
- TELESCOPES, SHIPS, COMPASSES TO HELP YOU FIND YOUR WAY
- DRAGONS TO SLAY, SHARKS OF SELF-DOUBT, REEFS OF FEAR THAT SLOW YOU DOWN
- GUARDIAN ANGELS, FISH OF LUCK, TREASURE OF GOOD FORTUNE TO SPEED YOU
- EARLY DISCOVERERS, LOCAL PEOPLE, GUIDES TO SHOW YOU THE WAY

A journey map gives us a lay of the land, even if we don't know all the details. Look at this road map from Today land to Future land as inspiration, then draw your own once you turn the page.

SHIPS OF
ADAPTATION
(WHAT TO KEEP,
WHAT TO LEARN)

GODSPEED
(PEOPLE +
THINGS TO
SPEED ME UP

JOURNAL
OF GRATITUDE

TODAY LAND

BRIDGES OF
DISCOVERY

TELESCOPE
OF "DO I SEE
MYSELF THERE"

LOCAL CLIMATE
(THINGS THAT
AGREE WITH ME)

TRIBES OF
PEOPLE (DO
I SEE MYSELF
AMONG THEM)

FUTURE LAND

TREASURES
(OF OPPORTUNITIES
TO BE FOUND)

FISH OF
GOOD LUCK
(UNEXPECTED
THINGS OF
GOODNESS)

ICONS +
SYMBOLS

When you're designing your life, it helps to express yourself in different ways. If your journey map is a visual expression, writing a letter is your written expression about long life. Deciding who the letter is addressed to is up to you—your future self, your kids, your partner, your hero. You pick! Give yourself no more than ten minutes to write your first draft. Go with your gut, and don't worry about making it perfect. You can always edit and refine it.

Verda Alexander is the Cofounder and Artist-in-Residence of the award-winning Studio O+A. Here is her letter to her future self.

DEAR ME — MY FUTURE SELF,
EMOTION — I AM FEELING SCATTERED, LIKE I AM
FLOUNDERING (IS THAT AN EMOTION?)
SUPERPOWER — I HAVE A GOOD CRITICAL EYE.
I CAN SEE THE BIG PICTURE AND THE DETAIL
SIMULTANEOUSLY. I CHALLENGE THE STATUS
QUO AND QUESTION EXISTING PERCEPTIONS.
CHALLENGE — I AM FINDING IT HARD TO
FIND FOCUS AND CLARITY IN WHAT MOST
EXCITES ME TO PURSUE NEXT.
OPPORTUNITY — MY OPPORTUNITY IS
THAT WE ARE IN A MOMENT OF GREAT
CHANGE, OF WHICH I HOPE TO BE A PART.
VALUE — MY VALUE IS I HAVE A KNACK FOR
SEEING WHAT NEEDS TO CHANGE AND
GETTING CREATIVE ON SOLUTIONS.
INSIGHT — MY HERO IS ME AND YET
MY PURPOSE IS NOT ABOUT ME.
NEXT STEPS — MY NEXT STEP IS
TO WRITE, SORT, ORGANIZE MY
THOUGHTS AND RESEARCH TO FIND
WHAT REALLY EXCITES ME AND SEE
WHERE IT TAKES ME.
WHAT EXCITES ME — POSITIVE CHANGE,
BY CREATING SPACES WHERE COMMUNI-
TIES SUPPORT ONE ANOTHER, VALUE HARD
WORK AND CONNECT TO A LARGER ECOSYSTEM.
BEAUTY, CRAFT, COMMUNITY, PURPOSE, PEACE.
I HOPE TO SEE YOU WELL + THRIVING IN THE FUTURE.

DATE _____

DEAR _____ .

1. SUPERPOWER: _____

2. KRYPTONITE: _____

3. VALUE: _____

4. CONSTRAINT: _____

5. OPPORTUNITY: _____

6. CHOICE: _____

7. EMOTION: _____

8. NEXT STEP FOR ME: _____
   _____

9. NEXT STEP FOR MY COMMUNITY: _____
   _____

SIGN HERE _____

DATE _____

DEAR _____ ,

1. SUPERPOWER: _____

2. KRYPTONITE: _____

3. VALUE: _____

4. CONSTRAINT: _____

5. OPPORTUNITY: _____

6. CHOICE: _____

7. EMOTION: _____

8. NEXT STEP FOR ME: _____
   _____

9. NEXT STEP FOR MY COMMUNITY: _____
   _____

SIGN HERE _____

DATE _____

DEAR _____ ,

1. SUPERPOWER: _____

2. KRYPTONITE: _____

3. VALUE: _____

4. CONSTRAINT: _____

5. OPPORTUNITY: _____

6. CHOICE: _____

7. EMOTION: _____

8. NEXT STEP FOR ME: _____
_____

9. NEXT STEP FOR MY COMMUNITY: _____
_____

SIGN HERE _____

DATE _____

DEAR _____ .

1. SUPERPOWER: _____

2. KRYPTONITE: _____

3. VALUE: _____

4. CONSTRAINT: _____

5. OPPORTUNITY: _____

6. CHOICE: _____

7. EMOTION: _____

8. NEXT STEP FOR ME: _____
_____

9. NEXT STEP FOR MY COMMUNITY: _____
_____

SIGN HERE _____

The user of this long life is you.

To bring your design ideas to life,
remember to have empathy for yourself.
What does having empathy for yourself
mean to you?

_____

_____

_____

_____

_____

_____

_____

_____

_____

_____

_____

_____

_____

_____

_____

_____

_____

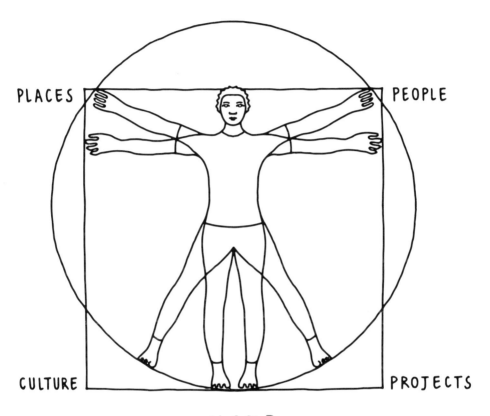

PLACES

PEOPLE

CULTURE

PROJECTS

USER
OF
MY LIFE

Design is a collaboration. Enlist collaborators in your designs. What is one thing you need help with as you design your long life? Instead of answering it yourself, which is harder to do, collaborate with your friends and ask them to give you ideas. This exercise is inspired by Marshall Goldsmith, renowned executive coach.

I need help with:

_____

Ideas from my collaborators:

1. _____

2. _____

3. _____

4. _____

5. _____

6. _____

I need help with:

_____

Ideas from my collaborators:

1. _____

2. _____

3. _____

4. _____

5. _____

6. _____

I need help with:

_____

Ideas from my collaborators:

1. _____

2. _____

3. _____

4. _____

5. _____

6. _____

What are some insights or "aha's!" you've had while using this journal? Draw, write, map them out.

_____

_____

_____

_____

_____

_____

_____

_____

_____

_____

_____

_____

_____

_____

_____

_____

_____

_____

_____

IT IS NEVER TOO LATE OR TOO EARLY TO DESIGN YOUR LONG LIFE!